1. Quaker, Quaker

19th Century Children's Chant

M.A.W.

2. There Was a Crooked Man

Children's Rhyme

3. Star Light, Star Bright

Children's Folksong

M.A.W.

Chimney Creek, 1988

4. Burny Bee*

Children's Folksong

M.A.W.

*Burny Bee is a Ladybug...the burning bee.

5. Sleep, Baby Sleep

English-American Folksong

M.A.W.

Chimney Creek, 1988

6. Old Mister Rabbit

Southern Folksong

M.A.W.

7. Lucy Locket

Children's Folksong

M.A.W.

8. Little Sally Rand

Children's Folksong

M.A.W.

4

9. I Climbed Up the Apple Tree

Children's Rhyme

M.A.W.

drm sl

do

I climbed up the ap - ple tree,

All the ap - ples fell on me.

Ap - ple pud - ding, ap - ple pie,

I climbed up the ap - ple tree,

Would you e - ver tell a lie?

I climbed up the

all the ap - ples fell on me.

Ap - ple pud - ding, ap - ple pie.

ritard.

ap - ple tree, ap - ple tree, ap - ple pud - ding, ap - ple pie.

Would you e - ver tell a lie?

10. Wee Willie Winkie

Children's Rhyme

M.A.W.

d m sl
drm sl

do

Wee Wil - lie Win - kie runs through the town.

Wee Wil - lie Win - kie.

do

Wee Wil - lie Win - kie, up - stairs and down - stairs, in his night-gown.

Rap-ping at the win - dow, cry - ing through the lock.

Are the child - ren in their beds?

Rap - ping at the win - dow. Are the child-ren in their beds, be - cause it's eight o' clock?

San Antonio, 1987

11. Grandma Grunts

American Folk Song

M.A.W.

drm s

2nd & 3rd Verses by M.A.W.

do

1. Grand - ma Grunts said a cur - i - ous thing.
2. Grand - pa Grunts said a cur - i - ous thing.
3. Un - cle George said a won - der - ful thing.

do

1. "Boys can whis - tle but girls must sing."
2. "Girls can whis - tle but boys must sing."
3. "All can whis - tle and all can sing."

For the students of Kritérion Montessori School, San Antonio, TX, 1988

12. Frog in the Mudhole

Children's Folksong — M.A.W.

13. Houn' Dog

Folksong — M.A.W.

14. Bought Me a Cat

American Folksong

M.A.W.

15. Rocky Mountain

Folksong

M.A.W.

Storm - y o - cean,_____ storm - y o - cean wide.

me. Storm - y o - cean,_____ o - cean wide.

When you're on that storm - y o - cean there's no place to hide. Do, oh, do, oh,

When you're on that storm - y o - cean there's no place to hide. Do, oh,

do re - mem - ber me. Do, oh, do, oh, do re - mem - ber me.

do, oh,_____ do re - mem - ber me.

16. Great Big House in New Orleans

Play Party Song

M.A.W.

drm sl
s,l, drm

do

Great Big House in New Or - - leans.

mi

Great Big House in New Or - leans, for - ty stor - ies high._____ Ev' - ry room in that big house

Great Big House in New Or - -

filled with pump - kin pie.

leans. Great Big House in New Or - leans.

Went down to the old mill stream to fetch a pail of wat - er. Put one arm a - round my wife the

Great Big House in New Or - leans, Great Big House in

oth - er 'round my daught - er.

New Or - leans. Great Big House in New Or - leans, Great Big House in New Or - leans.

Fare thee well my pret - ty miss, fare thee well my daught - er. Fare thee well my pret - ty miss with the

Great Big House in New Or - leans, Great Big House in New Or - leans. Great Big House in New Or - leans,

gold - en slip - pers on her.

Great Big House in New Or - leans. Great Big House in New Or - leans.

New Or - - leans.

Great Big House in New Or - - leans.

17. Blue

American Folksong

M.A.W.

d r m s

Here, Blue! Here, Blue!

I had a dog and his name was Blue.

Here, Blue!

I had a dog and his name was Blue. Here,

Blue! Here, Blue!

I had a dog and his name was Blue. Bet - cha five dol - lars he's a

18. Oh, Watch the Stars

Texas Folksong

M.A.W.

19. By'm Bye

Texas Folksong

M.A.W.

20. Shady Grove

American Folksong

M.A.W.

Most variants of Shady Grove are performed at a quick tempo. This setting should be performed at a slower, relaxed tempo. It is a study of seconds.
Think of a gentle wind whispering through the "Shady Grove". Compare with "Betty Ann", 2-Part American Songs, Book I.

San Antonio, 1977

21. Haul on the Bowlin'

Sea Chanty

M.A.W.